I0473862

THE
10 ESSENTIAL
STEPS TO
SALES
SUCCESS

Can You Benefit from the Wisdom
of a Successful Global 50 Sales
Executive? Absolutely!

Jerry A. Hering, MBA, Consultant

Table of Contents

Introduction

When I wrote "The 10 Essential Steps to Sales Success," I wanted to write a no-fluff book for business people looking to increase their sales success. Its aim was not to be long and esoteric, but full of practical and proven advice for anyone wanting to ramp up their wins in sales.

All the advice given here is based on my years as a sales professional for IBM and now as a consultant. Everything I list here has been personally used by me and key team members to increase sales and improve client relationships.

I hope this book not only inspires you but helps you improve your sales efforts whether you are a company owner, senior executive or simply what I refer to as the greatest job in the world, a sales professional.

Jerry A. Hering, MBA, President

ProfitMax Consulting, LLC

Step #1: Listen To The Client

Listen, Listen, Listen. Not listening correctly is probably the biggest error sales executives make that prevent them from making a sale. Too many sales folks are so eager to talk about their product or service that they fail to listen to what the client is saying about objectives, challenges or needs. As a result, the sales executive's credibility suffers and the client feels that the sales executive is more interested in making the sale rather than understanding the client's objectives, challenges or needs.

Listening skills are a combination of correct body language, eye contact and note taking. If you do these correctly, the client will know you are listening.

- ✓ *Body language*- your body language should adjust to your client's own body language and personality. The best approach here is to sit facing the client, not sitting with your legs to the side and torso to the client. Face your client with the whole body. Have a note pad or binder already in front of you and a pen ready to write.
- ✓ *Eye contact*- always make eye contact when the client speaks unless you are taking notes on a relative comment the client made. Nodding occasionally shows the client you are listening. Don't overdo the

nodding though as excessive nodding is a sign of insincerity.

✓ *Note taking*- only take notes on relevant points the client makes about a goal, objective or challenge. You should also take notes on any comments the client makes on new developments that pertain to the clients business, i.e. acquisition of a company, reorganization news, etc. Don't write down superfluous comments. Too much note taking can annoy the client and appear you are not listening.

A key validation point to the client that you are listening is to make a short relevant comment in response to a client comment. Once again: do not overdo this. Bottom line- you want to make sure the client knows you listened- and that can be validated by proper body language, eye contact and note taking. Unless you are giving a presentation or product or service update, the client should do most of the talking.

Step #2: Understand with Empathy

Always put yourself in the client's shoes. Most sales executives don't understand empathy- and lose opportunities because of it.

To get the empathy picture- you need to start by understanding each client's personality. Are they type A or B personalities? Do they have short fuses? Do they like or dislike small talk?

These are the kind of things you need to understand first with respect to empathy. As a meeting moves along, you need to pretend in your mind you are the client. How would you feel if you were the client as the meeting progresses? Is it going good or bad? If you understand how the client might be feeling, you will ultimately create a better outcome for any meeting. You may also be able to anticipate what might be coming from the client in the form of a concern, comment or gesture.

I use empathy primarily to anticipate possible anger or emotion that might detract from the sales effort. This potential anger or emotion can be mitigated by simply being aligned with the client's thinking.

One easy way to utilize empathy is to document the personality traits of each of your clients for periodic review.

Step #3: Get A Fast Start

Want to get off to a great start in a client meeting? Then dress appropriately (make sure you understand the client's dress code) and start with a firm handshake- but not a vice grip squeeze. If you have called the meeting- which is usually the case- size up the client's body language and demeanor quickly. If it is relaxed, spend a minute with small talk. If it is not, get right to it.

-   Thank the client for the meeting
-   Review the objective(s) of the meeting
-   Allow the client time to respond
-   Take relevant notes on important client comments
-   Close with an action plan regarding the meeting's discussions

Make sure you always respect the client's time. If the meeting was for 30 minutes, make sure you wrap it up within that time frame. If the meeting is going very well- and you can tell the client feels the same- then it may be appropriate to continue longer- ONLY- if you remind the client that the 30 minutes is coming to an end and politely ask if it is a hard stop. They will respect you for this as it shows that you know their time is valuable.

Step #4: Strategic Selling: Obtain and Sell To Objectives & Challenges

I consider strategic selling as selling to a client when there is no identified need for a product or service. Successful strategic selling separates the superstar sales executives from the mediocre sales executives. You are essentially creating the sales opportunity and validating it with the client rather than the client creating the opportunity via an RFP or email to you and your competitors. Strategic selling creates more sole source opportunities where you can preclude your competition from competing.

Strategic selling requires that you obtain your client's objectives and challenges. This is absolutely critical. I learned this approach while at IBM and used the methodology very successfully throughout my sales career there.

It is imperative that you ask your clients: what are their objectives for their business and subsequently, their challenges to achieve those objectives? Don't get goals and objectives confused. Goals are longer term visions you want to accomplish such as "I want to reduce costs". Objectives are specific and short term such as "I want to reduce costs by 12% this quarter".

Goals and objectives are often used interchangeably, but the main difference comes in their level of concreteness. Objectives are more specific and concrete, where goals are less structured.

The sales executive's goal is to sell their solution to satisfy the client's objectives. The first step is to obtain these objectives through a face to face meeting with the client. You will find that objectives are different among people within a client set. You need to document objectives by individual client. Once you have identified the key decision makers and their objectives and challenges- you can then create your solution from your product or service that will help them achieve those objectives (IMPORTANT NOTE: only ask for their top 2-3 objectives and challenges).

Once accomplished, you make the client a hero to their organization and consequently you become a hero to them because you provided the right solution that helped them meet their objective.

A couple things to know: make sure the meeting to obtain objectives and challenges is separate from the meeting where you sell your solution to meet those objectives and challenges. The reason is simple: you can't credibly sell a solution to a client's objectives/challenges on the fly. It takes preparation and maybe research, defining metrics, etc. so that you can validate to the client that your solution satisfies achieving the objective/challenge.

Here's an example of how strategic selling works: You set up a meeting with a key client decision maker so that you can understand their objectives and challenges for their line of business. Most clients will have no problem with this and appreciate the fact that you are trying to understand them and their business. Let's say one of their objectives is to reduce costs this quarter by 12%. You then ask what the challenges are for achieving this. The client responds:

> *"I may have to lay off a person and I don't want to do that"*
> *and/or*
> *"I already have a tight budget and not sure I can get to that 12%"*

So now you have the criteria to offer your solution via your product or service to help the client achieve their objective. Set a follow-up meeting with the client with the goal that you would like to show how your solution achieves their objective of reducing costs by 12%. Now it is up to you to be creative yet credible in presenting how your product or service will do that. Since I do not know your product or service- I can't be specific- but look at the benefits your product or service has provided other clients with respect to cost reduction and try and apply metrics (most credible) from that client to your client. Here are a couple of ideas:

- ✓ Present how your product or service has lowered operating costs, increased productivity, provided a quick payback, or an enhanced ROI and consequently reduced costs with other clients (try and quantify with actual dollars or as a percentage and reference the other clients)
- ✓ Offer a volume purchase agreement that will lower the client's cost if they purchase certain clip levels

Use this methodology to increase your sales dramatically.

Step#5: Tactical Selling: Obtain the "Win" Criteria

There will be many times when you will be asked to compete for an opportunity via an RFP, RFI or just knowing the client is competitively bidding the opportunity. This is a time when you need to make sure you follow a key protocol to allow you the best chance to win.

OBTAIN THE WIN CRITERIA.

Even if you receive an RFP or RFI, it is imperative you meet with the key client decision makers and ask them for their key criteria to win. Allow them to give you as many as they desire. Once they have offered this information, ask them to prioritize these as 1,2,3,.... Now you have the win criteria.

Take this information and ask the client for an opportunity to present your solution prior to the decision. What you want to do is present your solution- tying it to each of the win criteria. You may have three key decision makers with 3 different win criteria. Most likely, there will be overlapping win criteria from the three decision makers, so focus on the commonality of both the criteria and prioritization from the three.

It looks very credible to the client when you reiterate their prioritized win criteria (because it tells them that you listened) and show how your solution meets that criteria. As an example, let's say the client consensus on win criteria is warranty, price and functionality. Let's also say the consensus on priority of these is price, functionality and warranty. Start your presentation (preferably with all three decision makers in the room) by having them agree on your methodology- that the win criteria is price, functionality and warranty- and in that order. Once they agree, you can then show how your solution satisfies each criterion.

CLIENT WIN CRITERIA AND PRIORITY: HOW SOLUTION SATISFIED CRITERIA

- ✓ Price:
  30% discount off list with VPA clip levels
- ✓ Functionality:
  Multiple references, market share leader
- ✓ Warranty:
  5 years, best in industry

Use this methodology and you will close more sales opportunities.

Step #6: Obtain Client and Industry Knowledge

If you want to take your sales efforts to the next level-calling on C suite executives- then you will need to understand your client's business. This includes the organizational structure, financials (both P@L and Balance Sheet) and the executive decision makers. You will also need to understand the industry and the current industry dynamics i.e. merger activity, outsourcing, etc.

Use the web as much as possible to obtain:

- ✓ Company Data

- ✓ Annual Reports

- ✓ Press Releases

- ✓ Etc.

Also, use MarketResearch.com, Hoover's (a D & B company), and Standard and Poor's to obtain even more specific data on your client and industry. With MarketResearch.com and Hoover's, you can find current industry and client information that may be useful in your C suite meetings. Standard and Poor's offers financial-market intelligence and if your client is a public company, you can find in depth information on their stock.

Google of course, provides the easiest way to find information on your client and the respective industry they are in. This will be the best route for those not savvy in finance and financial acumen.

Take relevant points you have learned from your research and use them in client meetings where appropriate. You will look like a partner rather than a vendor. This strategy is a tremendous credibility builder for your sales success.

Step #7: Provide Competitive Differentiator

There will be many times when you are competing for a sale where all things are pretty equal with respect to your solution versus your competitor's solution. This is where you need to have or create a competitive differentiator. The differentiator can be very effective if it ties to the client's objectives and challenges criteria- so you need to really understand these criteria. Some examples could be:

- ✓ Longer warranty- ties to objective of enhanced customer service
- ✓ Better payment terms- ties to objective of enhanced P&L
- ✓ Volume discounts- ties to objective of enhanced P&L

It is important to note here that you also need to establish the "win criteria" first from the key decision makers. Make sure you meet the criteria before creating or providing the competitive differentiator.

Sometimes, the competitive differentiator is you- and that is good. This means that the client puts "value" in you- as a trusted partner to the client organization. This could be the result of a number of other things you offer including outstanding customer service, professionalism, or understanding the client's business, including their objectives and challenges. Usually, this value is earned over a period of time while calling on the client organization.

Make sure you work on creating a competitive differentiator as I won many key opportunities through this strategy.

Step #8: Provide Perfect Customer Service

Too many sales executives think customer service is a no brainer and very simple. They are wrong. Although customer service is not complex- it needs to be provided in the correct manner. Customer service can be entwined in any sales call of a new or established client. I found the following action plan to be most effective to ensure proper customer service and satisfaction.

- ✓ Send a succinct email to the client following a sales call. Thank the client for the meeting and synopsize the meeting, summarizing an action plan or follow-up plan using bullets. Use this approach with established as well as new or prospective clients.
- ✓ With established clients, ask them how you and your company are doing with respect to handling the account and meeting specific goals and objectives. Do this every 3 to 4 calls with this individual or group. Ask them specifically how you can improve service to them. Don't take any criticism personally- but make sure you listen and take notes on recommended areas of improvement. Make sure you implement these improvements ASAP.

✓ Do not send your client too many emails. You should only send emails that are relevant and provide value. Sending an email once a week to see how they are doing and to just say hi is usually perceived by most clients as a burden and waste of time. This approach can be a credibility buster. Your customer service credibility goes up when you send emails that are relevant to the success of their business- such as an article you read that pertains to their business or industry that provides new knowledge/insights into that business or industry.

✓ Set up one-on-one meetings every quarter with the sole intent to measure your customer service satisfaction with the client. Use a 1 to 5 scale (1 poor, 5 excellent) and ask them to rate you and your company on the following criteria:

  1) How are I and my company doing meeting your objectives?
  2) How are I and my company doing at providing value to your organization?
  3) How am I doing handling the account?

After every 1 to 5 rating, ask the client where improvement can be made. Subsequent to these quarterly meetings; send the client an email outlining an action plan for improvement including the action item, who and when.

Here is an example:

- ✓ Action Item

- ✓ Who Is Responsible

- ✓ Projected Completion Date

Customer service satisfaction can be enhanced by providing occasional social events for the client. This may include group lunches, dinners or group sporting events such as golf, baseball or football games. I found that once you build rapport with a client, and get them out for a social occasion- you then get to know them on a personal level. Once this happens, you will most likely see more sales and a closer partnership with the client that becomes more strategic, not tactical.

Step #9: Prepare Account Plans

You should do annual account planning for your clients and update them quarterly. Account planning really pays off as it gives you a map and protocol to follow with respect to opportunities, odds, and responsibilities. This is a great tool for reviewing with sales management as it shows that:

1) You are organized
2) You understand your clients
3) You understand the industry and most importantly,
4) You understand the sales opportunities.

The account plan is created for each client and should include the following:

- ✓ <u>Industry Overview</u> (obtain all information through Google research)
    1) *Growth*
    2) *% GDP*
    3) *Trends*

- ✓ <u>Client Overview</u>
    1) *Financials* (obtain through annual report, company website)

2) *Market Share* (obtain through independent research co's via Google)
3) *Key statistics* (obtain through annual report, company website)
4) *Revenue/Spending trends* (obtain from your IT department or sales admin)
5) *Business Initiatives* (obtain from annual report, company website and client meetings)

✓ <u>Key Client Wins</u> (last year's wins you closed)
✓ <u>Top Client Opportunities</u> (top sales opportunities you have identified)
✓ <u>Top Client Opportunity Analysis</u> (you create- see below)

1) *Opportunity*
2) *Revenue*
3) *Odds*
4) *Action Plan*
5) *Who*
6) *When*
7) *Inhibitors*

Follow this format to successfully manage and sell into your accounts.

Step #10: Have a Closing Strategy

A closing strategy is a creative way to show the client why they should do business with you rather than a competitor. It can be different with every client and every situation. You should make the strategy relevant to the opportunity you are trying to close.

You want to use it when you are delivering your final presentation and proposal. Make sure you have successfully utilized the criteria to win methodology and/or the obtain and sell to objectives and challenges methodology first. This should usually include a competitive differentiator- but it is not mandatory.

Once you have tied your solution to the client's objectives or win criteria, close with a "value add" that essentially will put you on top.

Examples of closing strategies that I have used that worked well are the following:

- ✓ Offer the client a free company resource for "X" days to assist in implementing your solution
- ✓ Offer a money back guarantee in the first 30 days if not satisfied with the solution
- ✓ Offer a longer warranty than is standard

Closing Thoughts

If you have comments or questions about "The 10 Essential Steps to Sales Success, I would like to hear from you. Please forward them to me at: info@pmaxllc.com

Furthermore, if you or your organization is interested in knowing more about ProfitMax Consulting or working with us, you can reach me at the following contact points:

Phone 503-226-3793

info@pmaxllc.com

www.pmaxllc.com

Thanks again and "Good Selling."